Let this book help you ~~~~ re
and Attend Co
Dream Big And ~~~~ High..!

2018

Starr Essence

GUIDE ME TO COLLEGE

GUIDE ME TO COLLEGE

10 VITAL STEPS EVERY URBAN YOUTH NEED FOR COLLEGE

Starr Essence

© 2017 Starr Essence
All rights reserved.
ISBN-10: 1546900764
ISBN-13: 9781546900764
Library of Congress Control Number: 2017910768
CreateSpace Independent Publishing Platform
North Charleston, South Carolina

This book is dedicated to:

Every person who inspired me to reach back and help those who would listen.

ACKNOWLEDGMENTS

FIRST, I WOULD like to give thanks and honor to God. My parents Nylene and Donald Watson who allowed me to make mistakes in my youth and gave me room to learn from my mistakes and accomplishments. Their discipline and love taught me not to settle for less than my heart desires of true happiness. My grandmother Gloria Cartwright for sharing her wisdom and life experiences to encourage me to strive for the best. My grandmother Hallie Allen (RIP) who shared stories with me about the power of networking. My great-grandparents Inez and Emmanuel Houston (RIP) for showing me the importance of faith and family. A special thanks to all my mentees who allowed me to be their mentor. Lastly, I want to thank all my mentors, family, and friends who pushed me to follow my dreams.

CONTENTS

A Message from the Author · xiii
Introduction · xvii

Phase One   **Preparation** · 1
Step 1   Why Is College Important For—YOU · · · · · · · · · · 3
Step 2   Do Your Homework—RESEARCH · · · · · · · · · · · · 9

Phase Two   **Planning** · 17
Step 3   Let Others Pay For College—SCHOLARSHIPS &
              GRANTS ·19
Step 4   Create A Strategic Success Plan—GRIND · · · · · · · · · ·24
Step 5   Beware Of The Big Bad Wolf—DEBT · · · · · · · · · · ·29

Phase Three **Progress** · **35**
Step 6   Create A Level Of—CONFIDENCE · · · · · · · · · · · ·37
Step 7   Actively Seek Your #1 Best Friend—INTERNSHIP · · · · · ·41

Phase Four   **Perseverance** · **47**
Step 8   Pay No Attention To Haters Or Naysayers—
              PERSEVERE ·49
Step 9   Be Connected—NETWORK · · · · · · · · · · · · · · · ·53
Step 10   Keep Yourself Accountable—JOURNAL · · · · · · · · · · ·58

              Epilogue ·63
              Sources, Permissions & Notes · · · · · · · · · · · · · · ·67
              Scholarship Resources · · · · · · · · · · · · · · · · · · ·73

"You learn valuable information and skills in college, but how much of that information is shared in grades K-12 to prepare you for college? Success in college is more than just high grades; it includes: branding strategies to compete in a changing job market, learning entrepreneur skills, acquiring scholarships and grants, and building a network of people who can help you in the process. "

- Starr Essence

A MESSAGE FROM THE AUTHOR

THERE'S QUITE A bit of discussion, and even some debate, on how to get urban youth into college. It's not that urban youth do not want to go to college; the problem is that they lack strategic guidance and understanding of the enrollment process as well as what it truly entails in completing a degree program. As a youth advocate and mentor, I've noticed that students are not being fully equipped with the tools to ensure their collegiate dreams come to pass. From the poorest neighborhood in Newark, New Jersey to the richest one in Los Angeles, California, students are being encouraged to attend college. However, there's an apparent gap in college preparation in our education system between African-American students and other races. In fact, even decades after Brown vs. Board of Education, the American educational system is still separate and unequal. Textbooks, computers, and educational enrichment programs are often obsolete in schools within African-American neighborhoods (i.e., urban school districts). It doesn't take a rocket scientist to figure out that there's an inequality issue in the education system in America. For example, I once visited a school in my hometown of Detroit, Michigan. During my visit, I recognized the poor maintenance and facility conditions at one school. There were holes in the walls, classrooms were guttered and abandoned, water fountains were undrinkable, and bathrooms were unusable, to say the least. I was in awe. I couldn't believe that in 2016, students in America had to learn in such challenging and uninspiring conditions. One thing I must say about that school, however, is that the library was magnificent. This observation, however, created another question for me, which was, *how often does the library get used?* If you take inventory in a public school in Detroit, and then take inventory of a public school twenty miles outside of Detroit, you will notice that there's a significant difference in the culture, educational resources, equipment, and tools accessible to the students.

Let's first look at the term urban and define it. What is urban?

1. Being or relating to cities and the people who live in them
2. Denoting or relating to popular dance music of black origin.

Who do we refer to when we mention the term youth? Youth is the time of life when someone is young—the time when a young person has not yet become an adult (i.e., a teenage boy or girl). Therefore, urban youth are children under the age of 18 who live in cities or areas that are primarily of black origin.

You owe it to yourself as an individual, particularly those who reside in inner cities, to Prepare, Plan, Progress, and Persevere as you transition to new levels in your life. Inner cities are not just comprised of African Americans, but of people from all walks of life, including race, culture, class, religion, and ethnicity. Statistics show that by 2022, the growth of Hispanics students will increase in primary and secondary public schools in America to 33 percent from 2011. Multiracial students are projected to grow even faster, to 44 percent. Is the American education system prepared for this growth? The American education system doesn't cater to most students in equitable fashion. Unfortunately, the gaps in educational success will continue to be problematic for urban youth, especially if the same educational opportunities and resources aren't equally distributed. It's not a white or black thing, it's an American issue that needs to be resolved if American students, holistically, are to succeed globally.

In some urban neighborhoods, youth are poorly prepared when it comes to the attainment of requirements and skill sets that are essential to obtaining a college degree. Not having access to resources and information to obtain higher education can be challenging for inner city youth. This is not to say that their goals aren't attainable, but it is to state that students who live in the inner cities tend to have to study and work harder than others. The academic expectations of African-American youth are lower than their counterparts. Factors such as parents' lack of school participation, lack of educational programs, student's low self-esteem, low-income households, and poor attitudes all contribute to the educational challenge for urban youth. But just how do we change this daunting plight? We change it by preparing, caring, loving, and guiding youth on the right path to success. It's no secret that every school in the United States of America has a different culture, academic curriculum, financial budget, administration, resource bank, variety of tools and activities, diversity pool, and the list goes on. If the curriculums aren't in unison, it becomes increasingly difficult to evaluate each student on the same standardized test such as the Scholastic Aptitude Test (SAT) and American College Testing (ACT). Some schools are more resourceful, advanced, technical, and socially equipped than others. Many urban schools lack essential information and programs to prepare their students for life after high school, which includes college. These barriers affect student poise, confidence, enthusiasm, self-fulfillment, career path, business skills, and lifestyles.

Let's face it, the education *system isn't fair.* Youth in Atlanta, Harlem, Washington, DC, Philadelphia, Milwaukee, New Orleans, Chicago, Memphis, and any other urban city in America might be at a disadvantage based upon their geographic location. Some school systems in these cities are biased. Their pedagogic processes (teaching methods) only cater to the A- and B-average students. So much for the C and below students, who are often left behind to fend for themselves, except for student athletes who seem to have more support, not because of their academic fortitude, but because of their athletic fortitude. But this book doesn't discriminate against A-, B-, C-, D-, or even F-average students.

The information shared in this book is geared to inspire, prepare, and push all students to reach greater heights, especially those students who live in urban America. **Applied information is POWER!**

My goal is to challenge every student who reads this book to become their best self. By following the 10 steps outlined in this book, students of all grade levels, high achievers and low achievers, will learn how to prepare for college. As they further their education, they will be motivated by their internal drive to reach even higher levels of achievement. This book serves as a guide to those who plan to attend college, while at the same time, gives them practical tools to use as they transition to adulthood.

INTRODUCTION

PREPARING FOR COLLEGE can be an exciting, intimidating, and overwhelming experience. In fact, planning for college is an act of hope and inspiration. It can also be an act of fear and rejection. Some students go to college as a means of breaking generational cycles of poverty, illiteracy, and lack thereof. Others are motivated by following the footsteps of their parents, grandparents, siblings, or some other role model. Today, it is instilled in young students to go to college as a precursor to success. The purpose of this manual is to provide parents and youth who live in urban areas with the vital steps in preparing for college and tips to ensure college success.

Listed are six basic questions and key considerations that help ensure success in college. These questions begin with the words taught in elementary school—Who, What, When, Where, How, and Why.

1. Who can mentor me as I transition into college?
2. What does it mean to attend college for my present and future state of being?
3. When is it best to start researching the college I want to attend?
4. Where should I go to college—Community, Technical, Private or Public College/University or an HBCU (Historically Black Colleges and Universities)?
5. How do I excel in my field of study during and most importantly, after college?
6. Why is attending college important?

Some students in urban neighborhoods are uninformed on how to properly prepare for college, which ultimately puts them at a disadvantage. It is, however, quite the contrary for those who reside in non-urban districts as well as those in other countries. For these groups, they are taught at an early age on how to develop efficient math, reading, and writing skills, which ultimately help enrich their college experience, while urban youth continue to lag socially, academically, and professionally. But if given adequate resources and tools, I believe urban youth can improve their standardized test scores and enhance their college experience. Standardized tests are used to measure a student's academic competencies. Obtaining a high-test score and meeting core admission requirements for the college of your choice is pivotal. According to a published article in The Huffington Post, when taking the ACT (American College Testing) and SAT (Scholastic Aptitude Test), one test is not better or holds a greater standard than the other. Passing standardized tests with sufficient test scores can increase one's chances of being accepted into a major college or university. Success for these students extends past the college experience. Students who are academically and socially equipped for college have a greater chance of succeeding in their careers as well.

It is my opinion that a collaborative and equitable education system combined with the assistance of mentors, parents, teachers, and programs can assist urban youth in properly preparing for college at an earlier stage as opposed to a later one. It is time that we teach our youth earlier about their college options instead of waiting until high school. Financial preparation for college is just as important. Not only does academic achievement play a major role in attending college, but financial education and support is imperative—scholarships and grants are helpful. Being awarded a significant amount of scholarship and grants can position students to attend college at reduced costs, and in some cases, for free. The time to reposition urban youth for success is now! In this book, we will discuss 10 vital steps that will remove barriers that hinder student success in college preparation and graduation completion. Adhering to these 10 steps will unleash the student's God-given potential through these four essential phases—**Preparation, Planning, Progress,** and **Perseverance**.

PHASE ONE

PREPARATION

WHY IS COLLEGE IMPORTANT FOR-YOU

"Before anything else, preparation is the key to success"

– Alexander Graham Bell

"By failing to prepare, you are preparing to fail."

– Benjamin Franklin

"Believe in yourself and in your dreams."

– Unknown

IN FIGURING OUT why you should go to college, ask yourself some simple, yet serious questions. The questions below will help jog your mind:

1. Why is going to college an intricate part of my life?
2. What benefits can I receive from earning my college degree?
3. Who can I inspire by going to college?
4. How can I position myself for success?
5. Where can I work nationally or globally with a college degree?
6. When should I attend college?
7. How much am I willing to invest in my college education?

8. Is it best to wait a few years or attend college following high school graduation?
9. Can I start taking college courses while I'm in high school?
10. Am I ready to attend college?
11. Do I want to get involved in a fraternity or sorority?
12. Should I go to a college in a location where I have friends and family?

Understanding why you want to attend college is the most important consideration because when challenges come, and they will, you must have the will power, passion, and drive to finish what you started. Understanding your reason why is imperative to your college journey. The journey you choose is yours, and only you can alter the outcomes. It is at this juncture in this book that I'd like to share a story with you as a perfect illustration.

There was a young girl from Detroit, Michigan who was excited about going to college. She was very outgoing. She held honors throughout her high school education and was a part of the National Honor Society. She graduated with a 3.5 GPA (grade point average) and was in the top ten percentile in her class, ranking number 13 out of 356 students in her graduating class. When she was in the tenth grade she wanted to attend college, but she was indecisive about her college choice. As a young girl, she always wanted the best things in life. She dreamed that one day she would own several companies and be wealthy. College was important to her, and she knew it would help her succeed in life. She decided to attend an HBCU (Historically Black Colleges and Universities) tour during her senior year in high school. Her parents supported her decision and paid for the college tour. As with this student, having a support system is valuable. Remember, not one person in this world has ever achieved success on their own.

Exploring her options for college was an eye opener for this young girl. The college tour she participated in consisted of Clark Atlanta

University, Spelman College, Morehouse College, Southern University, Alabama State University, Tuskegee University, Fisk University, Xavier University, Dillard University, Hampton University, Howard University, Tennessee State University, and Florida A & M (Agricultural and Mechanical) University. During the tour, she made up her mind that she would not only be the first in her immediate family to go to a university and move out of state, but she would be the first to graduate. Her reason for going to college was bigger than her—she wanted to change her family history. And she did just that. You see, you must decide if you want to step out of the box. Sometimes to be great you may have to walk alone. When making life-changing decisions, you will often be pushed out of your *comfort zone*. Most of her friends from high school stayed in Michigan and attended Michigan State University, Eastern Michigan University, or Ferris State University. The young lady in the story, however, decided to attend Tennessee State University for various reasons. She wanted to accomplish the following:

- Leave the environment of which she was familiar
- Make her parents proud
- Change her life for the better
- Show others how to follow their dreams
- Attend a HBCU, unlike any of her family members

In essence, the young lady in the story was ready to soar like an eagle and leave Detroit. What she wanted in life was more than where she was or where she grew up. Taking a leap of faith at the age of 17, she moved more than 500 miles away from her family and friends to attend college. It turned out to be one of the best decisions she had ever made. From that day forward, her life was totally transformed. In fact, she graduated from Tennessee State University and started her first telecommunications business at the age of 21. At age 25, she was a first-time home owner. In that same year, she followed her passion, and started her second business, a 501c (3) tax-exempt organization called *MorningStar International, Inc.*

I was that young girl. I grew up on Detroit Eastside in a single parent household until I was nine. I am no different from most urban youth. My biological father was killed in a senseless act of crime just months before I was born. I have always sympathized with youth who have lost a parent, and in some cases, both parents due to violence in the community in which they lived. I was blessed to experience both lifestyles of having one parent and then having two parents when my mom married my dad (stepdad). Looking back on my childhood experience, I can clearly see that God blessed me with both parents at the most sensitive and valuable time in my life.

Throughout my K-12 education, I managed to get good grades, for the most part. However, when I attended middle school, I became very rebellious. I became influenced by my environment during my pre-teen years. I hung around all the wrong people and did things that a child my age should not have done, such as skipping school. I skipped school to attend skip parties because it was considered the cool thing to do, so I thought. I've been in situations where I had to make decisions that would not only affect me but my family as well. At the time, I made poor decisions. I skipped school so much that Detroit Public School Board threatened to take my mom to court because of my excessive absences. I didn't want to see my mother get in trouble for choices I made. When I was in the sixth and seventh grades, I earned B's, C's, D's, and even some F's. Those grades did not reflect how intelligent I was, but it did describe my behavior and attitude toward school at that time. At some point in the seventh grade, I made a choice to do the right thing and get back on track. When it was time for high school, I wanted to attend one of Detroit Public School's top-ranking schools at that time. These included Renaissance High School, Cass Technical High School, and Martin Luther King High School. But my middle school transcript caused me not to be accepted into any of these schools. However, my test scores did allow me to be accepted into the next best school, which was Murray-Wright High School. I was also accepted into the accelerated college preparatory program. I wanted to go to Cass Technical High School originally and follow my mother's footsteps, but it didn't happen. Instead, I ended up following my dad's (stepdad) footsteps and graduated from Murray-Wright High School. I earned good grades throughout high school and participated in several organizations. I was selected as class vice-president and made great accomplishments during my high school years.

Using my own life as an example, we can be mindful that as teenagers and adults alike, we all have choices, and each choice can have good or bad consequences. Determined to continue the right path, I made a good choice in high school and decided to attend college, just like you can do. My high school counselor helped me by giving me waivers for my college application fees. My counselor didn't do that for everyone; he only helped those students who had potential or those who demonstrated effort and were eager to attend college. Having my own personal drive to go to college and the support of my family, friends, mentors, and teachers motivated me even more to pursue my goal. Remember, you are creating your own story. YOU must decide on why YOU want to go to college. Make sure the college YOU choose has a story that is connected to who you are or who you want to be. I chose Tennessee State University because I felt a strong connection to the culture and the people at the school during my college tour. I could relate to the student body. I felt comfortable and I knew in my heart that TSU was the college I would attend. In other words, it just felt right. When you get to college, you must always remember why YOU decided to go there in the first place. Start with the end results or goals in mind. Your reason *why* is the very thing that will push you along when you feel like giving up. Keep moving forward and watch your college dreams and life plans come to fruition. Don't quit on YOU!

TIME TO REFLECT: STEP 1: KNOWING WHY COLLEGE IS IMPORTANT FOR-YOU

In discovering why college is important to you, you should write down a short mission statement as to why college is important. What does it mean to secure a college education? Is your reason for going is to impact others? How are you going to pay for college? Believe in yourself and watch your plans transpire.

DO YOUR HOMEWORK—RESEARCH

"Academic success depends on research and publications."

–Philip Zimbardo

"Imagination is the highest form of research."

–Albert Einstein

"Research is formalized curiosity. It is poking and prying with a purpose."

–Zora Neale Hurston

TODAY, STUDENTS HAVE access to a ton of information due to internet accessibility and various social media outlets. But somehow college freshmen students are less prepared for college, as it now takes the average college student five years to graduate instead of the standard four years. Why? Because most college students are not mentally equipped or financially prepared for college. With this being the case, about half of freshmen college students are required to take remedial and/or developmental courses, due to low placement scores. These developmental and remedial courses are a prerequisite and must be taken before you can enroll in collegiate level courses. The real downside is that remedial and developmental courses are offered at regular tuition cost. In college, students most likely will "pay" for being behind academically. In addition, remedial and developmental courses are not credited toward the student's major. Students enrolled in these courses are basically paying for a course to teach them what they should have learned in primary education (i.e., K-12). And this is especially true for African-American college freshmen. However, if students are provided with adequate academic tools and resources it can help eliminate the pressure of trying to test out of remedial and development courses. It can be frustrating for a student if he or she needed to prolong their graduation date and hope that they have the funding to cover the cost. As we can see, preparation is valuable. ***Completing*** your education is essential to your success, as one of the main reasons why students drop out of college is due to lack of academic preparation and financial support. Knowing how to use accessible tools and resources such as Money Smart Publications can aid you in the process. Preparing for college is vital. Accurate information is essential to ***completing*** your college education.

This step will guide you in your research to attend the college of your choice. Most students depend on their parents to assist in this process, which is helpful, but the student is the primary person who should gather information. A barrier for many is not conducting adequate or sufficient research, which aids in ensuring whether college is truly a good fit for them. Obtaining updated information about tuition cost, acceptance rate, room and board, fees, book expenses, housing deposits, academic prerequisites, student population, financial aid, student culture, graduation rate, drop-out rate, default rate, job placement rate, student to faculty ratio, female to male ratio, major (concentration) and degree requirements, GPA requirements, and extra-curricular activities is valuable in your college success. This information is very important because it will help you jump start your college research. This may be overwhelming, if this is your first time learning the true ins and outs about college preparation. But don't get weary.

This information will help you now and in the future. Before we move further in Step 2, at some point you should ask yourself whether you are mentally, physically, spiritually, socially, emotionally, financially, and academically ready for college. And it's okay if you're not. Most college students aren't ready, but those who stay focused on their goals graduate from college with honors and/or sufficient skills. The real question is, have you studied or taken the SAT or ACT to measure where you are academically? Are you a good test taker or a poor test taker? Knowing your learning style and how to gauge your thought patterns is an advantage. Most people identify their learning style in graduate school or while in their careers. But if you learn it now, you are ahead of the curve.

You can take a free learning style quiz on the internet. Various companies have online education preparatory assessments. A list of some of these assessments can be found in the back of this book in the Resources section. These assessments will help you to understand your learning style, depending on how you answer each question.

Believe it or not, it's not too early for students in middle school to prepare for college. Middle school students can study to take the ACT test. Approximately 40,000 middle school students (6th–8th grade) take the ACT every year. If you are 13 years old or older, you can take the ACT, but you will need to study, review, and practice before taking the official ACT test. Sixth through eighth graders who take the ACT test can have their scores omitted if they score too low. The advantage of taking the ACT during middle school is to gauge where you are academically and to be considered for scholarships by Ivy League universities. It is highly recommended that parents and/or guardians purchase a SAT or ACT study guide when their child is in the sixth grade, particularly for those students who plan to attend colleges with elite programs, such as Stanford University, Harvard University, and Yale University. High school students should check with their school administration office to confirm whether funds are allotted for ACT or SAT Prep classes and the test. Most schools will pay for the ACT and/or SAT test one to two times a school year during a student's sophomore, junior, or senior year in high school. Students from urban communities typically take the ACT or SAT once or twice during high school, compared to their counterparts who take these tests at least three or four times while in high school.

More importantly than just taking the test is being prepared to take the test. However, most urban youth are unprepared to take either test. Studying for college admissions tests such as the ACT and SAT is crucial. But these are just some of the more notable tests. Some colleges and universities require students to take a placement test, regardless of their SAT and/or ACT scores. On the contrary, some colleges and universities omit having to take the college placement test if the student scores sufficiently on either SAT or ACT. It is important to note that some colleges do not require students to take the SAT or ACT, which is why researching your college of choice will save you time and money. Being proactive can save you from unexpected disappointments, so you shouldn't wait until the last minute to perform your due diligence. And not only do you research the school of your choice, but you should also take adequate inventory of yourself.

Questions to ask yourself:

- What are my interests, goals, and aspirations for the future?
- Where do I see myself (career path and lifestyle) in the next 5 to 10 years?
- What is my personality type? (You can search the internet for free personality test for teens.)
- Can I handle being away from my family and/or friends for a long period of time?
- How do I handle pressure and/or problems?
- What are my studying habits?
- Do I enjoy learning from people or from my own experiences?
- What are the top five colleges I want to attend?
- What are my strengths and weaknesses?

When understanding your interest, goals, and aspirations you should consider knowing your passion. Merriam Webster Dictionary defines passion as, "a strong feeling or enthusiasm or excitement for something or about doing something." Knowing your passion can help you master a skill and earn a profit or a paycheck from it. In researching your field of study choose a subject that you are passionate about. In addition, it will guide you toward a career that you can be proud of as well as be happy working in. While selecting the most beneficial career for you, it will not hurt to know your personality type. According to Myers-Briggs Type Indicator (MBTI), when analyzing your individual personality type, you may be surprised as to what is discovered. Researching this type of information can assist you in selecting the type of company you want to work based on your personality type. It is beneficial to understand how your personality fits into a company culture or environment if you want to grow with that company or if you want to work for yourself. To encourage you, I researched my personality trait and behavior as well. The dimensions of my MBTI are in four dichotomies of the following combinations—extraversion, introversion, sensing, intuition, thinking, judging, perceiving, and feelings. When I took the MBTI to assess my personality type, I was defined in an INFJ category—introverted, intuitive, feelings, and judging. This test is most accurate on the definition of my personality trait. I know that I am a person who looks for insight from a deeper source such as my spirit. I also care about people and their well-being. This test is based on how you answer each question.

Your personality and self-evaluation can give you a sense of how you deal with pressure and problems. Do you run from problems or do you face them head on? When studying for midterms or final exams, do you cram or pace yourself to retain information? Pacing yourself when studying a subject is best, because most of the time, you can retain the information better. If you cram you may know the information temporarily. You may forget everything you crammed shortly after studying it. A piece of good advice is that if you need to study but don't feel like it, study in a group. Never be afraid to join a study group. Learning from others can be a good experience. Being open to various types of learnings styles are beneficial during and after college.

It's quite all right to research various colleges, as it will arm you with options. Select your top five colleges you want to attend because every college is different. I remember a young man from Ohio who wanted to attend college. He enrolled into a four-year university. However, during his first semester, he decided that college wasn't for him. He dropped out of college his freshmen year and never came back. Therefore, it's important while conducting your own research to be sure to review the dropout rate of the colleges you might want to attend. This, of course, if the drop-out rate is important to you. Keep in mind also that even though you might drop out of school, you are still financially responsible for repayment of any loans you take out. When you sign a promissory note, you are required to pay that loan plus interest. Identifying your strengths and weaknesses will help you to identify the areas you need to work on. You will discover new things about yourself. Completing a personal self-evaluation by identifying your strengths, weaknesses, opportunities, and fears will help you discover what college best fits your needs and wants. Collecting information about yourself and the college of your choice can increase overall personal satisfaction. When researching your top five colleges, a little golden nugget of advice is to be sure to gather information on the areas highlighted in this section. If finding a job is your primary focus, then you need to research job placement rate for the college you plan to attend. If the college you attend has a low job placement rate and you value job security, you're going to be disappointed if it takes one to two years to find a job in your field. When you make an investment, you expect to get a return on your investment sooner than later. In the same vein, if you value high academics, make sure you select a university or college with outstanding accredited programs and affiliations.

Some schools are accredited and others are not. Let's discuss Morris Brown College as an example. Morris Brown College was founded in 1881 and lost its accreditation in 2002. Morris Brown still has students who attend the college, even after having lost its accreditation. According to The Journal of Blacks in Higher Education, Morris Brown College lost their accreditation due to an unstable financial position. The loss of their accreditation meant that students attending that college could not receive federal financial aid to pay for college. However, Morris Brown is still open and trying to regain its accreditation status. The U.S. Department of Education defines accreditation as recognition that an institution maintains the standards necessary for its graduates to receive admission to other reputable institutions of higher education or to achieve credentials for professional practice. The purpose of accreditation is to ensure that education on all levels provided by institutions of higher learning meets acceptable levels of quality assurance. By attending an accredited institution, it solidifies the quality standards that will be provided by an institution.

As you research the college of your choice, you will identify schools such the University of Chicago, Wharton University of Pennsylvania, and Princeton University that have robust academic programs and requirements. These private institutions look for the brightest and most academically-prepared students to attend their colleges. Private institutions are known mostly for their elite programs. In most cases, these institutions programs have 90% job placement rates. As well, public institutions like University of Michigan, Georgia Institute of Technology, University of Texas, and University of California-Berkeley have elite programs. As an example, according to *Money Magazine*, Georgia Institute of Technology's (Georgia Tech) industrial engineering program ranked #1 for the last 20 years for public colleges and universities. In addition, Georgia Tech ranked among the top 25 colleges when it comes to its undergraduates obtaining a 6-figure salary career without attending graduate school. This same school ranked #10 for business majors. The academic profile for Georgia Tech 2016 freshmen class is grade A on a 4.0 GPA scale, the average SAT's score ranged from 1330 to 1490, and ACT scores ranged from 30 to 34. As a student considering attending college it is imperative that you utilize your resources such as the Internet, teachers, parents, mentors, librarians, books, and community centers to assist you. Don't give up on <u>YOU!</u>

TIME TO REFLECT: STEP 2: DO YOUR HOMEWORK-RESEARCH

Identify the top five colleges of your choice. Do not research the school your mom, dad, teacher, preacher, or friend wants you to attend. If you are going to do yourself any justice, you should research the college you desire to attend. As a tip, research areas of importance in this section. Once you collect all necessary data, list the pros and cons for each school. Aim to master the requirements for your top three colleges. Apply to your top five colleges.

PHASE TWO

PLANNING

LET OTHERS PAY FOR COLLEGE-SCHOLARSHIPS & GRANTS

"A goal without a plan is just a wish."

–Antoine de Saint-Exupery

"Plan your work and work your plan."

–Napoleon Hill

DID YOU KNOW only about 20,000 students out of approximately 21 million who are expected to attend American colleges and universities receive a scholarship? Shocking! The great thing is you are now in position to prepare and apply for grants and scholarships because of the information shared in this book. More students can receive full scholarships if they are informed, equipped, and given proper assistance to apply for these funds. However, you must put forth effort to apply for various scholarships and grants. You cannot depend on someone else to do it for you. Interestingly, most students are afraid to apply for scholarships due to rejection, fear, lack of resources, lack of discipline, or no support. As a result, they end up with a significant amount of student loan debt after their college graduation. We will talk more about student loans in Step 5.

Applying for scholarships and grants provides a financial benefit because it allows you to know the type of financial support you will need to pay for college. We will talk about Federal Financial Aid in Step 5, which you will learn about your expected family contribution (EFC). Your blessing could be one scholarship or grant application away. Developing and improving your skills can increase rewarding outcomes in school and in life. Specifically, when you sharpen your skills in comprehension, reading, and writing you will begin to open doors for opportunities. Sharpening your skills and positioning yourself to be better every moment can solidify a debt-free college experience. Submitting A-1 qualities with each scholarship application can seal the deal. Having a tutor, participating in writing clubs or getting involved with writing programs and/or classes can increase your chances. Writing an essay for scholarships doesn't sound cool but being awarded a one hundred-thousand-dollar or a million dollars in scholarships is cool. I challenge you to change the status quo and become a competitive writer. Let your friends follow your footsteps and have a friendly competition by seeing who can get the most scholarships for college.

As a student, you need to understand that hard work and smart work pays off, but lack of discipline will cost you more in the long run. If you are afraid to apply for scholarships and grants due to the unknown, be encouraged – *YOU* can do it. Life is full of unfamiliar situations and circumstances, but the key to them is to face them head on and rise above them. You must overcome obstacles when you are planning on going to college. Do not be intimidated by the application process when seeking scholarships and grants. Some scholarships require you to write an essay while others do not. But never let essay writing steer you away. Start applying for as many scholarships as possible early in the college preparation process. It will help you overcome some of your fears because you will start to receive positive results—you will start to build self-confidence, and eventually, you will be awarded a scholarship.

There are several types of scholarships you can apply for. They include but not limited to: The Gates Millennium Scholarship, Coca-Cola Scholarship, Left Hand Scholarships, United Negro College

Fund Scholarship, Thurgood Marshall Scholarship, Urban League Scholarships, and First-Generation Student Scholarships. When applying for a scholarship you may need to write an essay of some sort. Creating a habit to write or improve writing skills earlier in your education can make it easier to apply for essay-based scholarships. Enhancing your writing and reading techniques, while strengthening your vocabulary can increase your chances of being awarded scholarships. Essay writing can be a turn off for most young people, especially those who procrastinate, but even those students are often gifted and smart. Personal essays give you an opportunity to express who you are and your desires. Some students do not like writing essays because it's time consuming or whatever the reasoning. There was a time when MorningStar International, Inc. a nonprofit youth organization, decided to give their MorningStar Scholars an opportunity to compete for a scholarship. Not one student applied for the scholarship in the first year. When the students were asked why they didn't apply for the scholarship, they shrugged their shoulders, indicated that they didn't have the time, or admitted that they didn't know where to start.

In college, some students cringe their teeth when the professor says write an APA or MLA paper. Most students, including collegiate-level students, do not like writing essay papers. But they do it anyway. You should improve and change your mind set about reading and writing. The Department of Education National Center for Education Statistics found that the average twelfth-grade African- American student reads at the same level as a white eighth-grade student. This statistic shows that African-American students are behind in Language Arts skills, which suggest that they're behind in other subjects as well. *Remember, reading is fundamental; learn to love it.* It's time to change the academic trajectory of your life. And to do so, you must **Be Prepared!** I challenge each parent and student residing in urban neighborhoods to invest in their education. Read more, study more, learn more, and demand more resources to ensure proper development. Don't forget, you need scholarships and grants to minimize cost in college. It takes an average college graduate three to nine months' post-graduation to find professional work, if they're lucky. For others, it may take longer.

In 2015, there was a college graduate who stated that it took her three years to find a career in her field of study in Atlanta, Georgia. She was an African American. In the land of opportunity (America), why is it hard for educated African Americans with a college degree to find sufficient work with matching compensation? Today, the job market in Atlanta, Georgia is highly competitive, especially for educated African Americans. The job market today, which is intrinsically tied to educational preparedness, is very different from the job market twenty years ago. Statistics from a 2015 research project found that in Atlanta, Georgia 22 percent of African Americans were unemployed, which is twice the overall city rate of 13 percent. The Casey Foundation in Atlanta reported that the graduation rate for black and Hispanic/Latino students in Atlanta Public Schools are at 57 percent and 53 percent, respectively, while the graduation rate among white and Asian students stood at 84 and 94 percent, respectively. According to the report, black and Hispanic/Latino students are highly likely to drop out. "Atlanta appears to be thriving, but it's clear that many of its residents of color, especially children and youth, are being left behind – to everyone's detriment," stated Kweku Forstell of the Casey Foundation. The purpose of this book is to guide you as you prepare for college and adulthood. With more people educated and information accessible, jobs can be difficult to obtain and maintain due to technology and automation. Residing in a specific geographic location can have an impact on what jobs are available. As students and future leaders of America, you need to be aware of the options available to you. We have been taught that going to college is necessary if you want to learn a specific skill or work in Corporate America. Obtaining a college degree can provide more, or in some cases, better opportunities for you, but learning a skill is powerful, too. For example, a college graduate with a finance degree in 2016 can earn a salary of approximately $55,000 (according to payscale.com), and a person skilled as an electrician can earn a salary of approximately $57,560 (according to salary.com). These are examples of options available to you as future leaders of America.

Throughout this book, you will read the words **Be Prepared**. *Preparation* is a process. In the process, you must make sure you *Plan*. When you plan, and execute your strategy you will begin to see *Progress*. Transitioning from high school to college is a paradigm shift to elevate your learning and your life. Continue to *Persevere* regardless of the outcomes, good or bad, until you see your goals and dreams transpire. Don't quit on <u>YOU</u>!

TIME TO REFLECT: STEP 3: LET OTHERS PAY FOR COLLEGE-SCHOLARSHIPS & GRANTS

You have homework. Apply to at least three to five scholarships and/or grants once a month. The more you apply, the greater your chances of receiving a scholarship. Remember, you can apply for scholarships and grants beginning in the eighth grade up through your senior year in college.

CREATE A STRATEGIC SUCCESS PLAN-GRIND

"An investment in knowledge always pays the best interest."

–Benjamin Franklin

"Never depend on a single income. Make an investment to create a second source."

–Warren Buffet

COLLEGE IS THE place where you develop and master a skill in your field of study. It is also a place that teaches you about running a business, as some colleges even have entrepreneurship programs. While attending college, it is necessary to find ways to make legitimate money. Most students drop out of college because of lack of financial support or resources. If finances pose an issue for you, it is necessary to work on your passion and G.R.I.N.D. At the end of Step 3, it mentioned the purpose and importance of jobs and described how the job market can impact your life. Well, creating a source of income on a college campus can be beneficial in many cases. This book mentions the word "GRIND." My definition for grind is **G**enerate-**R**eal-**I**ncome-**N**o-**D**elay or, in other words, hustle. Grind means to **be prepared**, **plan accordingly, proceed forward, and produce results.** Today, people never know when they will lose their main source of income and everything they have. Having a side job, business, or positive legal hustle is necessary, especially for college students. Many people have lost their jobs or their primary source of income due to company downsizing, corporate layoffs, outsourcing, or poor management. So, it's never too early or late to start your hustle— G.R.I.N. D!

Do you know the story of Russell Simmons? He went to college at City College of New York. However, he didn't complete his education. He decided to leave school to work in his passion—music. In pursuing your passion and discovering your purpose, it often comes with a cost. His parents wanted him to finish college, but college wasn't in his strategic success plan. He didn't have the enthusiasm to pursue his college degree, instead he became an entrepreneur in the entertainment industry. He was what they called a Hip Hop head. Russell Simmons went against all odds and decided to follow his passion and his purpose. He dropped out of college and strived to embark the Hip Hop revolution and the rest is history. It wasn't easy, but it was worth it for him.

Music artists such as Kurtis Blow and Run-D.M.C were founded by Russell Simmons. In 1984, he and partner Rick Rubin founded Def Jam Recordings, creating the foundation for the Cultural Revolution known as Hip Hop. Def Jam signed the forerunners of the Hip-Hop movement, including the Beastie Boys, LL Cool J, Public Enemy, and Run-D.M.C. Russell was an ambitious entrepreneur, and he saw Def Jam as his Hip Hop empire. His Rush Communications Company also included Phat Farm clothing company, television shows, management companies, publishing, and an advertising agency. His movie production company produced films such as *Krush Groove* and *The Nutty Professor*. In 1999, he sold his stake in Def Jam Records to Universal Music Group for $100 million. In addition, he sold Phat Farm for $140 million in 2004.

While Russell story is very inspiring, it's a one-in-a-million, similar to many black boys aspiring to play in the NBA. Very few will make it. The completion of college and the lifestyle it affords is a more reasonable option for most people. Having a hobby that you're passionate about or a job that you decide to grind in, can open doors of opportunities for you. You must realize how important starting and graduating from college is for you. Graduating from college can help you succeed in a global economy. College can teach you about business and how to operate a business.

I want to also share a story with you about a guy named Eric Thomas (The Hip Hop Preacher). He was a high school dropout from Detroit, Michigan. He was also a homeless teenager. He wasn't homeless because his mother didn't care about him. When he was young, he let his pride, behavior and ego get in the way of a major decision, in my opinion. He got into an argument with his mother, and she kicked him out of the house because of his disrespect. Eric spent a couple of years homeless in the mean streets of Detroit. At the two-year mark of being homeless, he began to turn his life around. Eric Thomas attended college in Alabama and joined a group of young men who were speakers/debaters. Since his college days, Eric worked on his passion perfecting his speeches and connecting with his audience. Today, Eric Thomas is an international motivational speaker who encourages, inspires, and teach youth and adults to succeed in life regardless of past mistakes. One of my favorite quotes by Eric Thomas states, "Be faithful over few. Every single opportunity you get, I need you to Grind on the little stuff! Don't tell me you're going to be on the honor roll. Shut up! Go to work! And show me!" Why am I sharing this story with you? As students, you too will face situations that will route your life towards a certain path. It is up to you to make wise decisions that will position you to succeed. To help you understand the importance of grinding on your passion now and during college is imperative. Eric Thomas managed to turn his poor decisions into positive outcomes. His strategic success plan was to invest in other people by inspiring them to be better. Preparing for college financially as well as academically is imperative. As a college student, it's beneficial to have at least one source of income. I'm not talking about your Federal Financial Aid refund check or your care package, I'm talking about money you can generate. Young women can create additional income by developing a product or service to market on campus. This includes becoming a stylist, crafting jewelry, tutoring other students or starting a small business. There are options for young men as well. You can start a youth business magazine, cut hair, mentor young boys, blog, or even design t-shirts and hats like investor, Daymond John. Daymond John did not go to college, but he became an entrepreneur. He started the fashion clothing line FUBU. The FUBU brand started with a $40-budget, and now it's a $6 billion brand. Daymond is a philanthropist, co-star/co-host on the television show Shark Tank, motivational speaker, investor, and best-selling author, to say the least. Daymond John is one in a million. The reason I'm sharing his story is to encourage you to work on your passion and establish income while you're in college. You never know what opportunities or threats may come your way. Please do not think I'm encouraging you to drop out of college, because that's the last thing I want you to do. However, what *Step 4* is conveying here is that it's smart to work on your passion and profit from it while attending college. Just think—athletes do it all the time. If you never heard of Daymond John, I encourage you to research and read his story.

Planning and saving for a rainy day will come in handy, especially when you least expect it. It's necessary to create a strategic success plan. In college, you may be faced with various obstacles and situations that will require some financial assistance. Securing enough financial aid, scholarships and grants to purchase books and classes is a must. If you do not pay for your educational expenses on-time you risk being purged. Purge is when the school drops all your classes if your tuition and room/board aren't paid in full by a given date. In addition, you may face a family emergency, a medical condition, an accident or natural disaster that may require you to leave campus immediately. Access to liquid assets or cash can help in those situations. Problems and situations don't care if you're a college student or not. They can come at any moment, at any time, and out of nowhere.

As a college student, you need to *be prepared* for the unexpected and GRIND always. GRIND in your books. GRIND in your job. GRIND in your passion. GRIND in your business. And G.R.I.N.D for a rainy day. Surround yourself with friends who have similar academic and life aspirations. Always work on your passion, because if you work hard, plan diligently, start small, and dream big, who knows you may be the next Russell Simmons, Eric Thomas or Daymond John from your city. Don't quit on YOU!

TIME TO REFLECT: STEP 4: CREATE A STRATEGIC SUCCESS PLAN-GRIND

List three things you do well that you don't mind working on for free. Then, list three things that you can produce that you believe people will buy. Compare the two lists and whatever product, skill or service you can provide on both lists GRIND in that area and make a profit in your passion.

BEWARE OF THE BIG BAD WOLF-DEBT

*"The rich rule over the poor, and the
borrower is slave to the lender."*

–Proverbs 22:7

*"The most important loan to pay is your student
loan. It's more important than your mortgage, car,
and credit card payments. You cannot discharge
student loan debt in the majority of cases."*

– Suze Orman

*"There are no short cuts to being debt-free. Get out of debt
the same way you learned to walk – one step at a time.*

– Dave Ramsey

IN AMERICA, MORE than half of college freshmen students receive federal student aid to pay for their college education. The application to apply for federal assistance is called FAFSA (Free Application for Federal Student Aid). When I speak to students throughout the United States, especially in urban neighborhoods, many of them want to attend college, but more than half of them do not know what the FAFSA acronym represents. Knowing basic information about paying for college is important. During your first visit, you will go on a college tour hosted by a college student or faculty member. Once they pique your interest, you will have an interview with a college recruiter, attend an open house or attend orientation, depending on the college you select. Most colleges will have a mandatory freshmen orientation for at least two days. You will learn the benefits of attending that college or university during your freshman orientation or from a college recruiter. In most cases, the cost of college is disclosed at the end of orientation. However, the staff and other representatives will make sure to emphasize all the gadgets, amenities, classrooms, computers labs, food courts, and so on prior to mentioning cost. This technique is to get you emotionally locked in first before giving you the 1–2–3 on financing your education. The 1–2–3 is loans, more loans, and other sources of funding. Be sure to apply for scholarships and grants outside of what the school offers. You want to graduate from college debt-free if possible. Did you know that only 39 percent of first time freshmen students attending 4-year public colleges/ institutions receive grants? More than 75 percent of first time, full-time undergraduate students received financial aid (loans). Financial aid consists of various types of aid from the federal government. If eligible, you can receive aid such as Subsidized and Unsubsidized Federal Loans, PLUS Loans (Parents or Guardian Only), Work-Study, Pell Grant, FSEOG, TEACH, and Iraq and Afghanistan Grants. Before receiving a loan, you will sign a promissory note indicating your promise to repay each loan.

Let's talk about avoiding the Big Mean Wolf—Federal Student Loans and any other loan, if possible. Most people attending college do not come from wealthy households or households with a significant amount of income to pay for college upfront. I encourage you to have a debt-free college experience. Why? Research found that after graduating from college, more than half of college graduates default on paying their student loans at least once. The reason is because most students have difficulty finding an adequate-paying job to help pay for their loans while supplementing for their lifestyle or living expenses. Ninety days after you graduate from college you are required to begin making payments on your loans. But you can start paying on your loan even before you graduate from college. Avoid defaulting on your federal student loans. You can default on your loans by not making payments 90+ days while in the repayment period, which typically begins post college graduation. Monthly payments are required but might not be affordable for some. Remember in Step 3, we talked about applying for large and small scholarships and grants because, ultimately, you can reduce or avoid student loan debt if you position yourself. Taking out a student loan is best if you don't have any other means to pay for your college education. Having a college education can improve the quality of life for most people. Taking out federal student loans may be necessary depending on the situation, but minimizing debt is a must in the process. The interest rate on federal student loans is low compared to many other types of bank loans.

Hear me clearly, if you need a loan to help subsidize your college education, you should consider a Federal Student Loan, not a private loan. If you believe that going to college will add value to your personal and/or professional growth, then I recommend that you only borrow what you need and not a penny more. **DO NOT** take out more than what you need. Taking out more than what is needed for college to receive a refund will cost you triple or even quadruple in the long run. When I was in college, I had two friends who didn't have any student loan debt when they graduated. Both received a four-year scholarship. One was awarded the Bill Gates Millennium Scholarship, and she attended Tennessee State University. The other received The Presidential Scholarship, and she attended Clark Atlanta University. Both were from Detroit, Michigan. When I completed my undergraduate studies, I had $22,000.00 worth of student loan debt. As a student, it is your duty to apply and receive as many scholarships and grants as possible to avoid the *Big Bad Wolf.* It is said that we all must make an investment to obtain a college education, but nobody told us how to invest in that same education using someone else's money. It is vital that you understand the importance of making an investment for college using other people's money to ensure that when you receive your degree, you walk the stage at graduation debt-free. I know you're thinking how do I attend college using other people's money? Scholarships and grants and more scholarships and grants, is the answer. How do you get scholarships? By applying, studying, increasing your writing techniques/skills, reading, playing around less, networking more, and actively seeking new opportunities that will pay for your college education. Positioning yourself academically and being involved in programs and youth associations can help you gain access to scholarships that wouldn't normally be available to you.

Some organizations and programs only give scholarships to their members or participants while other scholarships are available to all who meet the requirements. Parents can also help minimize the cost of college by starting a scholarship fund for their child with their financial institution. Minimizing student loan debt as much as possible can save you the headache of financial entrapment. More than 80% of working Americans who signed a promissory note accepting a federal student loan and/or private are still paying that debt 10 to 40 years later. The sad thing is that most of them studied in a major that they aren't currently working in. According to CNN Money, more than 40 million people in America have acquired an average of $29,000 in student loans, leaving United States of America with $1.2 trillion outstanding debt. Being prepared early in life can prevent unwanted college debt and career disappointments. Regardless if you're working in your career field or not, you are still responsible to pay back student loans to the federal government and/or private lenders. If you don't learn anything else in Step 5 understand avoid loans as much as possible. A more recent research finding indicates that the college graduating class of 2015 accumulated on average student loan debt of $35, 051 individually, Market Watch reported. To add a CNBC article, "The High Economic and Social Costs of Student Loan Debt," indicates that "The high levels of student debt are also serving to perpetuate and even worsen economic inequality, undercutting the opportunity and social mobility that higher education has long promised. Americans almost universally believe that a college degree is the key to success and getting ahead—and the data shows that, generally speaking, college graduates still fare far better financially than those with just a high school diploma." Don't quit on <u>YOU</u>!

TIME TO REFLECT: STEP 5: BEWARE OF THE BIG BAD WOLF-DEBT

Remember, scholarships and grants can minimize or eliminate student loan debt. List five financial resources or support that can help you avoid the Big Bad Wolf of student loan debt.

1. _____

2. _____

3. _____

4. _____

5. _____

Answers A). Scholarship Fund B). Grants C). Scholarships D). Youth Programs E). Internship Programs F). Savings

PHASE THREE

PROGRESS

CREATE A LEVEL OF-CONFIDENCE

"Progress is impossible without change, and those who cannot change their minds cannot change anything."

–George Bernard Shaw

"Knowledge is better than wealth, you have to look after wealth, but knowledge looks after you."

– African Proverb

"Be humble in your confidence, yet courageous in your character."

– Melanie Koulouris

"Optimism is the faith that leads to achievement. Nothing can be done without hope and confidence."

– Helen Keller

Do you know who you are? Do you know why you were created? Are you easily influenced by your environment and/or situation? My guess is that many of you don't know who you are. The reason why is because more than half of the students I ask these questions to have to ponder their thoughts, often before answering with, "I don't know." Some students go to college with no identity—not knowing who they are or being aware of their purpose. Knowing who you are is important, even at an early age. If you don't have your own identity, society and the crowd you keep will define who you are. Discovering the true person behind the face is essential. Knowing who you are or close to it, can help you build a level of confidence that can assure progress. Eighty percent of people are in jobs they hate because they went to college and majored in the wrong field. Now they're trying to discover what they really want to do. It's hard for them to identify who they are and their purpose in life. They're working at a job to make someone else's dreams come true instead of their own. They hate going to work every day. This type of person didn't discover how to create a level of confidence while developing their character. The only way to really have confidence is to know who you are. It is essential to know your purpose sooner rather than later to develop a great quality of life. When I speak at different schools, I ask the question, "What do you want to be when you grow up?" I have found out that some students know what they want to be, but there's a significant difference in the level of confidence in achieving it. There's a high level of confidence in elementary school students versus high school students. Somewhere in between elementary and high school students tend to lose their initial enthusiasm, imagination, ambition, and confidence.

I want you to gain confidence within. This book will guide you in the process with the steps to reach your goals. You must work on building self-confidence, self-respect, self- morality, self-integrity, self-determination, and self- drive before, during, and after college. I challenge you to boost your level of confidence. Webster's Dictionary defines confidence as: *1. A feeling or belief that you can do something well or succeed at something 2. A feeling or belief that someone or something is good or has the ability to succeed at something 3. The feeling of being certain that something will happen or that something is true.* When you are confident in yourself and your abilities, the sky is the beginning of the limit. This relates to going to college with confidence. You need to make sure you select the best major, roommate, mentor, and college. When you know that you selected the best school, you have a sense of satisfaction and achievement. Selecting a college that compliments who you are enables you to focus more on obtaining greatness. Having a mentor and or a sponsor who has your best interest at heart can enhance your overall college experience and livelihood.

A mentor is someone who teaches or gives help and advice to a person who has less experience and is often a younger person. Mentors can give you golden nuggets that can change your life forever. A sponsor is an individual or entity who organizes and is committed to the development of a product, program, person, or project; in this case, we are talking about you, the person. Most people aren't familiar with having a sponsor until they're older. But if you can find someone who is passionate and dedicated enough in seeing your dreams transpire, I assure you that either a sponsor or mentor will benefit you. I know you probably heard the saying "anything worth having is worth fighting for." Please don't misunderstand what I am saying here. What I am saying is that having a mentor and/or sponsor can make your college and your life decisions a little easier. But don't think that any of your problems will disappear because you have a mentor and/or a sponsor. Stay humble in the process of who you are as well as who you desire to become. I encourage you to achieve your goal of attending college. You only win in life by moving forward with confidence and belief. It's time for you to Be Phenomenal! Don't quit on <u>YOU</u>!

TIME TO REFLECT: STEP 6: CREATE A LEVEL OF -- CONFIDENCE

Below list 3 people, dead or alive, who you would consider to be a mentor. Mentors do not have to be someone you personally know. They can be the president, author, activist, teacher, parent, friend, supervisor, or pastor. Now list 3 people who you can ask to be your sponsor. Remember sponsors are people who will invest in you, your program, project, or product.

Sponsors	Mentors
1.	1.
2.	2.
3.	3.

ACTIVELY SEEK YOUR #1 BEST FRIEND-INTERNSHIP

"A good name is better than wealth."

– African Proverb

"Find something you're passionate about and stay tremendously interested in it."

– Julia Child

"Be so good they can't ignore you."

– Steve Martin

THROUGHOUT COLLEGE, YOU will be exposed to career resources and tools through the Campus Career Service Center. Taking advantage of the resources and tools available to you at your Campus Career Service Center is extremely imperative to your professional success. In fact, maximizing your current skills now and during college will increase your chances of working in the field of your choice. The main thing that most adults regret after graduating from college is not getting an internship in their major. They end up like 80% of Americans who work in a job that they didn't go to college for, just to make ends meet. Not getting an internship, co-operative (Co-Op), or an externship while you're in college will put you at a disadvantage and behind the competition. Do you know the difference between an internship and externship? According to business dictionary, "An internship is a period of supervised training required for a profession. It follows a specified number of academic credit hours or classroom years. An externship is a training program that is a part of a course study of an educational institution and is taken in a private business. A Co-Op is when a high school or college students receives career training with pay throughout the academic year while working with professionals in their field of study. Remember that the world is flat. You are competing for career and business opportunities before, during, and after college. Don't be naïve and think because you have a 3.1 or 4.0 GPA, that you're not going to compete in your profession. To ensure you're able to improve the quality of your life here in America and globally, you must use all your resources to ensure success. Remember, one of your resources is community programs. An internship in the field that you're passionate about can lessen the headache of finding a job after college because you will gain real experience on the job. I learned of a young lady who was an accounting major and was offered an Internship with FDIC. It was a two-year internship program, meaning that it would prolong her graduation date. Instead of her graduating from college in four years, it would take her six years. In her mind, it was a good offer but she was apprehensive. She was determined to graduate from college in four years, and didn't even want to consider anything that would interfere with her pre-established graduation timeline. Even though, the opportunity could have added value to her life in many areas, she wasn't open minded enough to see the true value in the opportunity. She turned down the offer at FDIC. She was only looking at where she was at the time. Truth be told, it could have been the career to change her life for an even rewarding outcome. Luckily, the following summer she received an internship as a teaching assistant for NASA-SEMAA program, of which she received for two consecutive summers. In her junior year, she started to feel like she had made a mistake for not taking the FDIC internship opportunity. She felt that she made a poor decision. She continued to move forward with her accounting degree to graduate in four years. In between time, she started to feel overwhelmed as graduation was slowly approaching. In her junior year, she realized that she had no professional accounting experience. She heard about people who graduated from college with no work experience and couldn't find a job. Finally, the summer of her senior year she received an internship as auditor for the Tennessee Education Lottery Corporation. In that role, she felt like it wasn't enough to prepare her for the real world in corporate accounting. She then enrolled in an entrepreneurship program through the College of Business on campus. Upon graduation, she still felt like she wasn't equipped to compete with other accounting and finance professionals. She needed a career that could add significant financial and professional value in her life to compete in a global economy. Later, she learned that it was a mistake not accepting an internship with FDIC. After graduation, it took her 11 months to find a job related to accounting and finance, but it wasn't what she desired. Today, she's doing well as an entrepreneur. She still thinks about not taking that internship at FDIC.

However, knowing what she knows now about life, her goal is to empower, equip, and educate those who come after her about taking advantage of opportunities. She is working in her passion today by educating, guiding, and training youth to follow their passion through college and entrepreneurship. In fact, please note that after you graduate from college most companies want you to have at least two years of working experience in your field. If not, it can be challenging to find work in your area of study. Attending graduate school after receiving your undergraduate degree, can count toward your two years of working experience. Even if you decide to go to graduate school, please be sure to get an internship. I know you may be thinking, *"But I'm a freshman in high school or still in junior high. How do I gain working experience now?"* I recommend you volunteer at an organization to gain working experience and develop your resume. Some companies expect traditional undergraduate students to acquire working experience while going to school full-time. In my opinion, that's not realistic. That's why I am emphasizing the importance of having an internship, Co-Op or externship. Most traditional undergraduate students only focus on their academics, sports, music, or some other activity. Having a job while going to college is not a high priority for most. If you don't get anything out of this step, I hope that you understand the importance of obtaining an internship at some point before you graduate from college. Don't quit on <u>YOU</u>!

TIME TO REFLECT: STEP 7: ACTIVELY SEEK YOUR #1 BEST FRIEND-INTERNSHIP

Get an Internship! Your internship is your best-friend in college. Do not be misguided by the freedom to do as you please. You need an internship if you want to compete in America, better yet, internationally. Obtaining an internship with great benefits even if it prolongs your graduation date is necessary. In the end, it will catapult your career to new levels.

Name 10 places where you would like to receive an internship.

1. _____

2. _____

3. _____

4. _____

5. _____

6. _____

7. _____

8. _____

9. _____

10. _____

PHASE FOUR

PERSEVERANCE

PAY NO ATTENTION TO HATERS OR NAYSAYERS-PERSEVERE

*"Great works are performed, not by
strength, but by perseverance."*

−Samuel Johnson

"Life begins at the end of your comfort zone."

− Neale Donald Walsch

*"Perseverance is not a long race; it is many
short races one after the other."*

−Walter Elliot

"Without a struggle, there can be no progress."

−Fredrick Douglas

WHO DO YOU think of when you hear the word perseverance? Well, aside from my mother, I think of First Lady Michelle Obama. She demonstrates perseverance and she is a woman of character. Michelle Obama is no stranger to struggle and overcoming obstacles. She was born and raised in

Chicago (South Side), Illinois. Growing up on the South Side of Chicago, she wasn't privileged. She and her oldest brother shared close quarters where they slept in the living room, having a sheet to separate the two. Despite the conditions of their upbringing, obtaining a good education was emphasized by their parents. By the age of four, both Michelle and her brother knew how to read. Unlike some youth in urban neighborhoods today who are illiterate or read below grade level, Michelle and her brother were smart enough to skip the second grade. ***Remember, reading is fundamental. Learn to love it.*** In the sixth grade, Michelle was taking gifted program courses, and she learned French. Michelle graduated from High School as class salutatorian. In 1985, she completed her undergraduate studies in Sociology from Princeton University with Cum Laude honor cords. Thereafter, she studied law at Harvard Law School, and she was awarded her J.D. in 1988. She pursued her career in corporate law and in public services. In 1993, she held the position of executive director for the Chicago office of Public Allies, a nonprofit leadership training program. Michelle continued to tackle new endeavors, and in 1996, she joined University of Chicago as the associate dean of student services and worked in the University of Chicago Hospital as an executive director.

Michelle Obama's story is a very inspirational one, no doubt about it. But don't think for one second that First Lady Michelle Obama didn't have haters and naysayers. I'm quite sure she did. Even with naysayers or haters, what does it mean to persevere? Perseverance means to endure even through difficulty. Being resilient no matter what comes your way or who talk bad about you. Keep your dreams and goals in front of you. By having a determined spirit and a positive mental attitude you will be able to overcome many haters, obstacles, and issues in college or in life.

Every one of us will have haters or someone who will try to speak negative against us. No one person is any different from the other technically, but class, race, religion, creed, and cultures make us believe otherwise. People from all walks of life have haters, including youth. Haters are everywhere. If you start listening to haters, and believing what they say, then, you will fall into the trap of insecurity, not fulfilling your dreams. Let your haters be one of the driving forces to catapult your dreams and unleash your true potential. Use that energy to enhance your passion, grades, career, network, work ethic, net worth, business, and your social skills. Remember, haters will hate people from the slums to the mansions. In his song "Stay," Hip Hop Rapper Nas said it this way, when addressing haters— *"We enemies, but your hatred could never enter me, some seek fame cause they need validation, some say hatin' is confused admiration, spotlight on me, I still look twenty, still get money, lady killer pushin' a Bentley, maybe dudes could see too much of their failures through a dude who realer, I don't like you near bruh, but I need you to…. Stay."*

Nas is basically saying I know who I am, people need to know who they are. But instead some people hate on others because of their failures and poor work ethic. However, in the same breath, he's expressing that he needs his haters to keep hating on him. He uses their hatred to become his best self. If you're reading this step and think you don't have haters, I beg to differ, you just don't know it yet. There's all type of haters and naysayers from family to friends to classmates to teachers, or even to people you don't even know. Use the energy from those who hate against you to increase your success. College is the pre-game to the real game we call adulthood. Life after college is when you will become more aware of haters, more than ever before. Remember that there's not one course in college that teaches you how to overcome or even deal with those who are jealous or envious of you. But Life 101 can teach you how to overcome haters and naysayers. It is imperative that you use positive energy against those who hate against you. Strive for excellence in the midst of it all. Warren Buffet puts it this way, "Honesty is a very expensive gift. Do not expect it from cheap people." Strive to be better today than you were yesterday. Persevere and let your light shine bright regardless of the challenges that may come your way. Don't quit on <u>YOU</u>!

TIME TO REFLECT: STEP 8: PAY NO ATTENTION TO HATERS OR NAYSAYERS-PERSEVERE

Use your haters as motivators. Remember, every human being has at least one hater. Learn to use negative energy from haters and convert it to positive energy. Make your dream a reality. Never add negative energy to negativity, only fight it with positive energy to increase your overall success, whatever it may be.

Write down three positive strategies that you can use to persevere.

Example: I will work on my dream in some way shape or form every day for 30 minutes, no matter what.

1. _____

2. _____

3. _____

BE CONNECTED—NETWORK

*"You can make more friends in two months by becoming
interested in other people than you can in two years
by trying to get other people interested in you."*

– Dale Carnegie

*"Nothing liberates your greatness like the
desire to help, the desire to serve."*

– Marianne Williamson

SHOUT OUT TO my introverted and extroverted people, including youth. Both introverts and extroverts can benefit from networking, regardless of age. My introverts are those individuals who are energized by being alone; they like to have me-time. Whereas my extroverts are energized by being around people, they are social butterflies. In fact, at times you may possess both character traits. According to the Webster dictionary, "An introvert is a shy person: a quiet person who does not find it easy to talk to other people. An extravert or extrovert is a friendly person who likes being with and talking to other people: an outgoing person." Regardless of your trait, one of the key strategies today is networking with people from diverse backgrounds. Exposure to new things and people can position you for better outcomes. Exploring various youth programs, associations, and professional or social networks outside of your personal circle of friends can place new opportunities in your lap. In various networks or associations, you can discover professions and skills that peak your interest. Knowing the right people at the right time or the right people knowing you at the right time can lead you on a positive path towards a great future. What associations and/or organizations are you currently involved in to guide you towards personal development?

Listed below are areas to use for networking:

- Youth Programs/Associations
- Peer Leaders/Counselors
- Volunteering
- Recreation Centers
- Library Membership
- Fraternities/Sororities
- Student Activities
- Starting a business (Teen Entrepreneurs)
- Personal Blog (Social Media)
- Religious Youth Ministries
- Summer Youth Camps or Jobs
- College Work-Study Programs
- Externships and Internships
- Community Service

While networking, be sure to connect with the right organizations and the right people. Only align yourself with people who are where you want to be. Take advantage of people you know personally who are in elite groups. Utilize and appreciate free opportunities to network with people you don't know. If you want to be a teacher or start a youth organization, one of the first things you should do is volunteer at your neighborhood school, church, recreation center, a small non-profit, or youth club. These opportunities will position you to build networks with different types of people. Building your social clout and being strategic in the process is a win-win situation. Being able to communicate with people on various levels can build rapport and new relationships. Meeting new people on a consistent basis is a positive trait that is necessary when networking today. Not limiting yourself and keeping an open mindset will allow you to feel comfortable when networking with people. Use your network to grow your net worth while you're young. Building new positive and healthy relationships while forming a level of trust and respect, can build a large network of contacts. Networking with people who are genuine is a plus. People who really want you to succeed will help you get further faster. Building a network by volunteering at your favorite organization or local store is another good starting point. For example, volunteering at a business, organization or a church can help you develop certain skills sets while building your social skills and network connections. If you were to volunteer at a business, you will learn what it takes to operate that business. You will identify a group of people who you can learn from and share ideas with. When you volunteer with an organization such as a nonprofit you will develop skills on what it takes to be a social entrepreneur. You will have pride in serving others with a mission—in most cases bigger than you. Volunteering at your church can expose you to different areas of need in the ministry such as: hospitality, finance, video and broadcasting, dance, security, or an usher. And these positions require you to talk to people. Networking by volunteering for a business, event, or an organization can increase your social, professional, communication, and business skills. And with consistency you can change lives including your own. Who knows? You might get an offer to work or partner with an organization. There are truly no limits. You could even be the next Steve Jobs.

Speaking of Steve Jobs, let's talk about Apple for a second. Twenty-five years ago, people could care less about an Apple product. Apple has been in existence since 1976. However, in the last 20 years, Apple has experience a paradigm shift in their overall performance growth.

Now people stand in lines, or set up shop in tents to purchase their new Apple products or services. Consumers will patronize Apple retail sellers to purchase an iPhone, iPad, iWatch, or I whatever, just for the sake of being an owner of an Apple product. What if you had the opportunity to volunteer at Apple in their grassroots stage? Can you imagine where you would be?

Networking with people in your community is a start. What start-up company or organization in your local area do you think you want to volunteer for? I challenge you to write a letter to that company or organization about how you are interested in volunteering. In the letter, showcase your abilities and capabilities in a business letter format. Explain how they can utilize your skills. Write down what you can contribute to their organization as a volunteer with the skills or efforts you possess. When you get the volunteer position, don't forget to work diligently, hard, smart, and be efficient and effective in your assignment. Networking is not about what you can take from someone, but what you can give. Young leaders, remember that it's not all about who you know; it's also about who knows you. Don't quit on <u>YOU</u>!

TIME TO REFLECT: STEP 9: BE CONNECTED-NETWORK

Networking is essential when competing in a global economy. You are no longer competing with your friends down the street or in your class. You're competing with youth in China, Japan, Brazil, Germany, Italy, Spain, Denmark, Switzerland, and so on. The opportunities in America are more readily accessible now due to the advent of the Internet. Be sure to create a quality network of people you believe can help you and vice versa.

Below, list the three organizations / associations / programs that you are actively participating in. Then list three organizations / associations / programs that you want to get involved in.

1. _____

2. _____

3. _____

1. _____

2. _____

3. _____

*Network with MorningStar International, Inc. sign-up to become a MorningStar Scholar at www.reachastar.org

KEEP YOURSELF ACCOUNTABLE-JOURNAL

"A personal journal is an ideal environment in which to BECOME. It is a perfect place for you to think, feel, discover, expand, remember, and dream."

– Brad Wilcox

"Words are but pictures of our thoughts."

– John Dryden

"A man's mind, once stretched by a new idea, never regains its original dimensions."

– Oliver Wendell Holmes

IN THIS FINAL step, Step 10 will help you put things in perspective. I want to remind you of the importance of completing your college education, business venture, or whatever dreams you may have within. I highly recommend buying a journal and writing in your journal daily. College is one area that you should take time to write down your experience, goals and thoughts. In my opinion, it's more significant and valuable to capture your thoughts on paper or digitally. To journal means to record your life's greatest moments via paper, tablet, laptop or computer. Your college days will be some of the most amazing moments of your life. Recording your thoughts or ideas also helps you to become aware of your mindset. Tracking your thoughts daily brings awareness to your conscience and subconscious mind. You will be amazed at what you discover about yourself a year, five years or even twenty years from now. On your first day visiting a college campus, write down your experience. And then during your freshmen year of attending college, write down your daily experiences. You will be amazed at the moments you shared with your classmates. In college, you want to capture your goals or thoughts as well.

I know you might have heard the saying, "Write the vision, make it plain." Writing your vision helps you to be accountable to the goals, ideas, dreams, visions, and even thoughts that you desire at a moment in time. Sometime seeing what you wrote can be an electrifying force that pushes you even harder to achieve it. When your ideas or vision become a reality in the physical/tangible form, it can be one of the happiest moments of your life. Be encouraged to write every day. Some people think having a journal or diary is for girls and women, but I am here to tell you that boys and men can journal, too. Taking a moment in each day to write about what happened or to record your thoughts can bring great fulfillment, and sometimes, it can release stress. Keeping a journal of your life is smart. Writing in your journal can free your mind from unwanted tension. Trust me, I know this from my own personal experience. It can remind you of the goals you set for yourself. It can teach you how to think before you react while discovering your mindset at that moment. In life, aim to be intentional while making wise decisions, and you will live a balanced life. Reading your journal a few days, weeks or a month at a time can help you track your mindset. In college, having a positive mental attitude is an essential ingredient for peace within. We didn't talk a lot about having and keeping a positive mindset. Having a positive mindset will forever evolve you as an individual. I want to emphasize the importance of writing your plan, thoughts and ideas daily. I encourage and challenge you to turn your dreams into reality. Just how do you turn your dreams into reality? You first must believe in yourself and in your dreams and that includes both youth and adults. Then, write down your strategic success plan and goals. Create a personal mission statement to abide by. Honor your craft wholeheartedly. Work diligently by faith and know that the Almighty God is on your side. You do your work until it becomes manifested in the natural realm. Lastly, you must start journaling today. Don't quit on <u>YOU!</u>

Today, I _____

_____

_____

_____

_____

_____

_____

_____

_____

_____

_____

_____

_____

_____

_____

_____

_____

_____

_____

_____

TIME TO REFLECT: STEP 10: KEEP YOURSELF ACCOUNTABLE-JOURNAL

Your assignment is to journal for a complete 30 days, wait 30 days before you read it, and then, read Day1 of your journal. I challenge you to journal for a complete 30 days. Keep a record of what you discover about yourself. Don't forget to write daily.

EPILOGUE

IT IS MY hope that you, the reader, have heard my voice within the text of Guide Me to College: 10 Vital Steps Every Urban Youth Need For College. I wrote this book with hope to share information, to inspire, and with intentions to help prepare you for college and adulthood. You are the next generation of future leaders in this world. When I was younger, I didn't have access to the volume of information available today. So, I encourage you to always be proactive in whatever career path you decide to take. Remember, college isn't for everyone, but if you decide to attend college, please make sure that you graduate with a skill set that will make you marketable in a forever changing world. Use the wisdom shared in this book to help you make the best decisions in choosing the right college. You should identify why college is good for you first and foremost. Allow the research already done to help you in the process. Although I didn't specifically recommend that you purchase Barron's Profile of American Colleges (latest edition), I highly recommend that you do purchase this book, as it will provide valuable information and help guide your research. Being prepared essentially means that you should be proactive in conducting your own research surrounding the college you want to attend. Barron's profile will provide you with resources and data on specific colleges. The published information includes data on student population, tuition and room/board cost, programs, males vs. female ratio, etc. I want each of you to apply for as many scholarships as possible, regardless of big rewards versus small rewards or essay required versus non-essay required. In conducting research, don't forget about the significance of scholarships. Attending college for free with the help of scholarships and grants is better than paying for college out of pocket or with student loans. Remember, going to college doesn't guarantee an average or high paying job. The job market today is different compared to what it was twenty years ago. As an example, the unemployment rate among college graduates in 2015 was 7.2% compared with 5.5% in 2007. As we can see, the job market is changing and is becoming more competitive.

My goal in sharing much of this information is so that today's students can be more proactive than the 80% of American college graduates who are still paying off their student loan debts, nearly 20 years after graduating from college. Among other things shared in this book is the importance of having a mentor or a sponsor. It's never a bad thing to have someone who can guide and support you in the right direction in your future endeavors. For those who are determined to attend college but don't receive any scholarships or grants, know that it's okay to apply for federal student aid (FAFSA) to help pay for your college education. If you do not receive any or not enough scholarship and/or grant monies, student loans are an option. Participation in organizations and programs aside from school curriculum or program might provide additional aid to help pay for college. Full or partial scholarships are also available to those who participate in sports or play a musical instrument (music scholarships).

There is no one-path journey for all students. However, there are various resources that can help all students achieve an intended end—the attendance and completion of one's college education. One of the easiest ways to do this is to first start by identifying one's passion. Your passion is often intrinsically tied to purpose—the reason *why* you were born in the first place. With this in mind, know that it is possible to work on your passion and your college major simultaneously. When you identify your passion and purpose earlier rather than later, it can bring happiness to your life. Pursue your passion with confidence knowing that one day you can turn your passion into a paycheck. Working on your passion can allow you to receive income and save for a rainy day. You want to G.R.I.N.D in your passion while building a level of confidence, knowing that you have what it takes to be successful. At the same time, however, the skills you develop in your field of study in college will help catapult your career. Create a strategic success plan for college and your life. Consider obtaining an internship while in college. Obtaining an internship gives you actual experience in your career field while you are working towards earning your degree. This is crucial, as the distinct advantage of completing an internship makes you more marketable in the industry of your chosen profession. Most companies consider hiring recent college graduates with working experience immediately. Networking while in college is also a good way to help navigate one's career path. Meeting the right people at the right time is essential to landing a good job, in some cases. The geographic location can make all the difference with networking. It may not be what you know or how much you know but who you know or who knows you! Networking gives you a chance to socialize with different types of people while still in college.

Guide Me To College: 10 Vital Steps Every Urban Youth Need For College provides a wealth of information on being proactive in preparing for college as well as life beyond college. It is my hope that this book will be used as an empowerment tool to help students and parents build the bridge of success within their communities that other people can follow. In doing so, success can be duplicated for generations to come.

God bless every individual who takes the time to read, share, and follow Guide Me To College: 10 Vital Steps Every Urban Youth Need For College to obtain personal and academic success.

SOURCES, PERMISSIONS & NOTES

1. Hussar, W. J., & Bailey, T.M. (2014). Institute of Education Sciences (IES) National Center for Education Statistics: Projections of Education Statistics to 2022. (41st Ed). U.S. Department of Education (p. 5), Page 7

2. "Before anything else, preparation is the key to success" – Alexander Graham Bell www.brainyquotes.com, Page 14

3. "By failing to prepare, you are preparing to fail." Benjamin Franklin www.brainyquotes.com, Page 10

4. "Believe in yourself and in your dream." – Unknown, Page 10

5. The Truth About Standardized Tests: How They Affect Your College Application January 13, 2014, Updated March 15, 2014 by Kat Cohen www.huffpost.com, Page 8

6. "Academic success depends on research and publications." –Philip Zimbardo www.brainyquotes.com, Page 15

7. "Imagination is the highest form of research." –Albert Einstein www. brainyquotes.com, Page 15

8. "Research is formalized curiosity. It is poking and prying with a purpose." –Zora Neale Hurston www.brainyquotes.com – Page 15

9. http://www.educationplanner.org/students/self-assessments/learning-styles-quiz.shtml - Page 16

10. http://www.cbsnews.com/news/should-a-7th-grader-take-the-act-or-sat/ By Lynn O'Shaughnessy, September 4, 2013 Should A 7th Grader Take the ACT or SAT? Page 16, 17

11. Money Smart for Elementary School Students, Money Smart for Young People www.fdic.gov/education, Page 17

12. Merriam Webster Dictionary: Passion Definition, Page 18

13. Myers-Briggs Type Indicator Test http://www.myersbriggs.org/my-mbti-personality-type/take-the-mbti-instrument/, Page 18,19

14. The Journal of Blacks in Higher Education: Morris Brown College Emerges from Bankruptcy April 6, 2015 https://www.jbhe.com/2015/04/morris-brown-college-emerges-from-bankruptcy/, Page 20

15. http://www.gatech.edu/about/facts-and-figures, Page 21

16. "A goal without a plan is just a wish." –Antoine de Saint-Exupery www.brainyquotes.com, Page 23

17. "Plan your work and work your plan." –Napoleon Hill www.brainyquotes.com, Page 23

18. www.fafsa.ed.gov, Page 23

19. The Department of Education National Center for Education Statistics http://nces.ed.gov/, Page 25

20. "An investment in knowledge always pays the best interest." – Benjamin Franklin www.brainyquotes.com, Page 23

21. "Never depend on a single income. Make an investment to create a second source." –Warren Buffet www.brainyquotes.com, Page 23

22. Russell Simmons Biography http://www.biography.com/people/russell-simmons-307186

23. Eric Thomas http://etinspires.com/

24. Daymond John http://daymondjohn.com/

25. "The rich rule over the poor, and the borrower is slave to the lender.", Proverbs 22:7 New International Version https://www.biblegateway.com/passage/?search=Proverbs+22%3A7 – With Permissions

26. "The most important loan to pay is your student loan. It's more important than your mortgage, car, and credit card payments. You cannot discharge student loan debt in the majority of cases." – Suze Orman www.brainyquotes.com

27. "There are no short cuts to being debt-free. Get out of debt the same way you learned to walk – one step at a time, Dave Ramsey www.brainyquotes.com

28. https://lendedu.com/blog/student-loan-debt-statistics

29. CNN Money 40 Million Americans Now Have Student Loan Debt by Blake Ellis September 10, 2014 http://money.cnn.com/2014/09/10/pf/college/student-loans/

30. CNBC The High Economic and Social Costs of Student Loan Debt by Kelly Holland Monday June 15, 2015 http://www.cnbc.com/2015/06/15/the-high-economic-and-social-costs-of-student-loan-debt.html

31. 80% Hate Their Jobs--But Should You Choose A Passion or Paycheck? By Alyson Shontell http://www.businessinsider.com/what-do-you-do-when-you-hate-your-job-2010-10

32. "Progress is impossible without change, and those who cannot change their minds cannot change anything." –George Bernard Shaw www.brainyquotes.com

33. "Knowledge is better than wealth, you have to look after wealth, but knowledge looks after you." – African Proverb http://www.inspirationalstories.com/proverbs/t/african-on-money-wealth/

34. "Be humble in your confidence, yet courageous in your character." – Melanie Koulouris www.brainyquotes.com

35. "Optimism is the faith that leads to achievement. Nothing can be done without hope and confidence." – Helen Keller www.brainyquotes.com

36. Ecclesiastes 9:11 New International Version https://www.biblegateway.com/passage/?search=Ecclesiastes+9%3A11&version=NIV

37. "Great works are performed, not by strength, but by perseverance." –Samuel Johnson www.brainyquotes.com

38. "Life begins at the end of your comfort zone." – Neale Donald Walsch www.brainyquotes.com

39. "Perseverance is not a long race; it is many short races one after the other." –Walter Elliot www.brainyquotes.com

40. "Without a struggle, there can be no progress." –Fredrick Douglas www.brainyquotes.com

41. First Lady Michelle Obama Biography http://www.biography.com/people/michelle-obama-307592

42. Nasir Jones Song Stay "We enemies, but your hatred could never enter me, some seek fame cause they need validation, some say ha-tin' is confused admiration, spotlight on me, I still look twenty, still get money, lady killer pushin' a Bentley, maybe dudes could see too much of their failures through a dude who realer, I don't like you near bruh, but I need you to…. Stay."

43. "A good name is better than wealth." – African Proverb http://www.inspirationalstories.com/proverbs/t/african-on-money-wealth/

44. "Find something you're passionate about and stay tremendously in-terested in it." – Julia Child www.brainyquotes.com

45. "Be so good they can't ignore you." – Steve Martin www.brainyquotes.com

46. Business Dictionary: Internship and Externship Definition http://www.businessdictionary.com/

47. "You can make more friends in two months by becoming interested in other people than you can in two years by trying to get other people interested in you." – Dale Carnegie www.brainyquotes.com

48. "Nothing liberates your greatness like the desire to help, the desire to serve." – Marianne Williamson www.brainyquotes.com

49. Merriam Webster Dictionary: Introvert and Extrovert Definition

50. MorningStar International, Inc. www.reachastar.org

51. "A personal journal is an ideal environment in which to BECOME. It is a perfect place for you to think, feel, discover, expand, remember, and dream." – Brad Wilcox www.brainyquotes.com

52. "Words are but pictures of our thoughts." – John Dryden www.brainyquotes.com

53. "A man's mind, once stretched by a new idea, never regains its original dimensions." – Oliver Wendell Holmes www.brainyquotes.com

54. http://www.educationplanner.org/students/self-assessments/learning-styles-quiz.shtml

SCHOLARSHIP RESOURCES

1. Myscholly.com

2. Scholarships.com

3. Fastweb.com

4. ScholarshipPoints.com

5. Cappex.com

6. TheCollegeBoard.com

7. Niche.com

8. Chegg.com

9. Unigo.com

10. ScholarshipMonkey.com

11. Collegenet.com

Proceeds from this book will benefit MorningStar International, Inc. Youth Programs and Scholarships

For Booking Information, please contact:
Starr Essence
Email: Starressence26@gmail.com
www.starressence.com

Made in the USA
Columbia, SC
30 September 2017